"ZIG-ZAG"

The Hampdens of 420 (RCAF) Squadron, R.A.F.

January – August 1942

In accordance with the requirements of the Copyright, Designs and Patents Act 1988 Peter J Sainty has asserted his right to be regarded as the author of this work.

© Peter J Sainty, 2008

ISBN 978-0-9556933-3-5

All rights reserved. No part of this publication may be reproduced without the express permission of the publisher

Second Edition

The assistance given by the volumes mentioned in "bibliography" is acknowledged, as is that provided through many Internet websites. Of the latter, particular mention should be made of Internet postings made in 2007 by the family of the late Flight-Sergeant Jack Gibbs, RCAF, which allowed me to correct the official record in respect of his service.

Published by Peter J Sainty, 62 Ashbourne Road, Derby DE22 3AF through www.lulu.com

Cover photo: Handley-Page Hampden at dispersal, RAF Waddington, 1942. It is believed this aircraft is "Zig-Zag".

"ZIG-ZAG" – The Hampdens of 420 (RCAF) Squadron

CONTENTS

Page

420 Squadron – The "Hampden" period 7

Aftermath 31

Which aircraft was "Zig-Zag"? 33

In Memoriam 37

Prisoners-of-War 40

Citations 41

Aircraft loss records 45

Specification 51

Bibliography 55

Glossary... 57

Illustrations

Page 5 – Handley-Page Hampden in flight
Page 13 – Squadron photograph at Waddington
Page 14 – The aircraft with the ground-crew; aircrew
Pages 21 & 22 – Aircrew & Ground-crew group; Pilot, Navigator & Wireless Operator Groups; Wireless-Operator in flying suit.
Page 49 – Squadron signatures
Page 53 – 44 Squadron Hampdens over Lincolnshire

An early Handley-Page Hampden in flight, photographed from the wireless-operator's station of a similar aircraft.

This photograph gives a good idea of the narrowness of the fuselage.

420 SQUADRON – THE "HAMPDEN" PERIOD

420 (RCAF) Squadron ("Snowy Owl"), Royal Air Force, was formed, as part of 5 Group, Bomber Command, on 19th December 1941 at Waddington, just south of Lincoln, taking the place of 207 Squadron which had moved to Bottesford a month earlier, having been at Waddington since its reformation in November 1939. Also at Waddington was the veteran 44 ("Rhodesia") Squadron, which had been there since the beginning of the War, and which was now preparing for its re-equipment with the new Avro Lancaster, while it struggled against the loss of its popular Squadron Commander: on 13th December 1941, Wing-Commander Misselbrook, and all of his crew, had been lost without trace, flying on a minelaying mission in one of the aged Handley-Page Hampdens which 44 Squadron was about to hand over to 420.

The twin-engined Hampden had been designed to the same Air Ministry specification (B.9/32) as the Vickers-Armstrong Wellington, and both prototypes flew within a week of each other in 1936. But looking at the two aircraft side-by-side showed a striking contrast in interpretation of that specification. The Barnes Wallis-designed Wellington, affectionately nicknamed "Wimpy" after the character in the Popeye cartoons, was immensely strong and rugged: its geodetic "basketweave" construction became legendary for its resilience to damage. It had powered gun turrets in the nose and tail, complemented by a ventral turret (though the latter was later replaced by beam guns) and had a relatively wide fuselage which enabled all the crew stations to be easily reached, and, perhaps more importantly, crew members to exchange positions if necessary. It had the look of an aggressive war-machine. The Hampden, by contrast, looked frail and delicate - though happily this was something of an illusion, for the aircraft proved able to withstand substantial flak damage – with an incredibly thin-looking tail-boom which was apt to flex in flight, giving the uneasy impression that it could break off at any time. Breakage in the air was, thankfully, extremely rare, though it was not unknown for Hampdens to break their backs after being treated too roughly on the ground.

The Hampden's designers apparently envisaged a crew of five, with a navigator sitting on a cushion on the main spar behind the pilot, and the bomb aimer in the nose. However, the Air Ministry combined these two roles, reducing the crew to four (although a fifth was sometimes carried, to operate "special equipment", his place being rather claustrophobic-ally in the tapering section behind the main crew stations). The navigator/bomb aimer used the main-spar cushion on take-off, however, it being considered an unnecessary risk for him to be in the nose (and hence closest to likely accidents) until the Hampden was airborne.

The Hampden's armament consisted of a fixed gun ahead of (and operated by) the pilot; a moveable gun in the nose, operated by the observer/navigator; twin Vickers "K" guns mounted amidships behind the pilot, facing rearwards and operated by the wireless operator/air-gunner, and a similar arrangement below this, operated by the other rear-gunner. Enemy fighters soon realised the weakness of this arrangement, with the inevitable result that beam attacks were carried out with the primary aim of killing the pilot and thereby effectively crippling the aircraft; for the other main drawback of the Hampden was the narrowness of the fuselage, which severely restricted crew movement. In theory, a wounded pilot could be removed by lowering his seat backrest and pulling him back into the wireless-operator's station, allowing the observer/navigator to take his place; but there were hot debates as to whether this was actually possible in practice. There are documented cases where a wounded pilot was relieved by the navigator in this way, but equally there are cases where aircraft came to grief (or almost came to grief) when the manoeuvre was practiced; and in at least one case it is believed that this resulted in the deaths of the entire crew. The fuselage was only three feet in width, which effectively meant that the pilot, once in place, was stuck there for the duration of the mission (a problem graphically described in Guy Gibson's book *Enemy Coast Ahead*).

It was some time before a frustrated Hampden navigator unshipped his gun and fired at the enemy through his side-window. After that, some provision was made for beam guns, although operating these was still tricky in the cramped environment.

But the Hampden had its good points. It was generally acknowledged as a delightful aeroplane to fly, with handling characteristics verging on those of a fighter; indeed, at least one Hampden pilot accounted for an enemy aircraft by treating it exactly like that, dispatching the opposition with his fixed gun. It was nearly 20 mph faster than the Wellington, and had a range almost 300 miles better, albeit with a lower bomb capacity. Initially, both aircraft used Bristol Pegasus engines, though the Wellington later switched to the Bristol Hercules. The Pegasus was a radial engine of legendary reliability and the crews regarded them with a great deal of affection. Nevertheless, by 1942 it was generally recognised that the Hampden was outdated: while the Wellington went on to become the only bomber used in its original role throughout the war, the Hampden was already being removed from the bombing campaign, to be used by Coastal Command or for training. Exclusive to Arthur Harris's 5 Group (ironically, in view of Harris's widely-reported antipathy to all things Handley-Page), it was the mainstay of that Group in the first two years of the war, but by late 1941 few Squadrons still used it, as it was phased out in favour of, firstly, the unreliable Manchester and then the legendary Lancaster; and by the end of April 1942, only two front-line bomber Squadrons – 408 and 420 – used Hampdens, though Operational Training Unit (OTU) Hampdens occasionally took part in Main Force raids (crewed largely by instructors).

As well as its aircraft, 44 Squadron provided 420 with some of its personnel, most notably its first Commanding Officer. Squadron-Leader Joe Collier, DFC and Bar had been a 44 Squadron flight-commander, and was promoted to be the most junior Wing-Commander in the Group to take over the new squadron, which he did with immense enthusiasm and energy, determined to make 420 as good as 44. He was joined by other 44 squadron personnel: Squadron-Leader Wood became "B" flight commander in 420; and another one making the move was Sergeant John Timmis (known to his family as "Jack", and to his comrades as "Timmy"), at 27 an experienced Observer who came from Tunbridge Wells. Other squadrons, too, of course, provided personnel for the new Canadian squadron. From 83, that veteran squadron in which Guy Gibson had served at the outbreak of war, came the Canadian "A" flight commander, Squadron-Leader Campbell, and also the scholarly Pilot Officer Robert Rayne, a recently-qualified pilot and a former Oxford Blue. Still serving with 83 squadron on 9th January 1942, P/O Rayne had been acting as Observer (Navigator) in a Hampden during a night mission to Brest (it was customary for pilots under training to undertake a few missions as navigator to get them used to operational flying); on its way back to its base at Scampton in the mid-morning of the 9th, the Hampden had to make an emergency landing at Sedgebrook (not far from 5 Group Headquarters at Grantham), in the course of which the aircraft was wrecked. Fortunately all the crew escaped without injury. (The pilot of the aircraft, Sgt. Price, died less than three months later when the 83 Squadron Manchester he was flying collided with balloon cables near Sheerness, with the loss of all crew).

On his arrival at Waddington, P/O Rayne teamed up with Sgt Timmis, and also with a wireless-operator/air-gunner Sergeant named Norman Axford, another native of Kent, his home-town being Dover. These three were frequently photographed together, possibly because the other air-gunner was taking the pictures! – that fourth member of the crew was probably Sergeant John Elliott, about whom the official records are vague, though his Service number indicates he joined the RAF some months before Sgt. Axford. Sgt. Elliott was certainly with them at the end, and therefore it may be assumed that he was also with them at the beginning: in some squadrons the lower air-gunner was peripatetic, as that fourth crew position was used for training, with successful trainees going on to become wireless-operators/air-gunners in their own right; but the indications are that this was not the system used by 420 Squadron. But photographs of the entire air-crew confusingly show five members, and it has been impossible to identify which of the two "spare" sergeant gunners was Sgt. Elliott. (It is possible that the fifth crew member was a beam gunner).

They were allocated an aircraft which they christened "Zig-Zag". Unfortunately, neither the serial number nor the squadron identifying letter of this aircraft is known: it might conceivably have been "Z", giving rise to the name; equally, the name could have arisen from P/O Rayne's apparent penchant for taking evasive action as much as possible, referred to in a cryptic note from Norman Axford. They had the name painted on the nose of the aircraft, together with a map of Germany emblazoned with a swastika and being hit by a bomb. Crude in comparison to some of the intricate "nose-art" later applied to Lancasters and Halifaxes, it nevertheless no doubt gave a sense of ownership. (But 420 Squadron had its own "nose-artist" – Floyd "Skip" Rutledge from Doaktown, N.B., Canada, joined the Squadron in April 1942, and he painted the head of a native American, in full head-dress, on the nose of one Hampden. Later he moved on to some elaborate art-work on Halifaxes).

If the casualty records are representative, there were very few – if any – all-Canadian crews in the Squadron at this stage of the war: equally, there were only a few all-British crews. The crew of Zig-

420 (RCAF) Squadron, 1942 – RAF Waddington
(see also page 49)

"Zig-Zag"'s Ground Crew posing with & working on the aircraft

The Aircrew: ?, R N Rayne, N F Axford, J H Timmis, ?
Sgt. Elliott is assumed to be one of the men on the extreme right or extreme left of the group, but it is not known which, nor is the identity of the other known.

Zag was all-English, and one other crew listed among the casualties comprised three Englishmen and a Scot. F/Sgt. Johnson, the pilot of that crew, was not far from home, for he came from Cleethorpes.

Wing-Commander Collier had much to contend with. Many of the ground crew provided by 44 Squadron were those who 44 was only too pleased to see the back of; tools failed to arrive; and the age of the battle-scarred Hampdens naturally gave rise to several problems. However, by 21st January 1942 all was ready, and the Squadron, the Hampdens proudly bearing "PT" squadron codes in place of 44's "KM", set off on its first mission to Emden. It was not an unqualified success. Squadron-Leader Wood, flying his precious new Hampden "S for Sugar", failed to return – a particularly severe blow to Wing-Commander Collier, who could scarcely believe that he had lost his friend and Flight-Commander on the very first operation. Happily, some time later the Squadron received the news that all four crew members had survived, albeit as prisoners-of-war. They believed their aircraft had been hit by flak, but it was claimed by Ofw. Rasper of II/NJG2 that he had brought it down.

Trips to Münster and Hannover followed, and also another attack, on the last night of January, on the capital ships in the "hot-spot" of Brest. There were also the regular minelaying missions, but there were no further losses for 420 during this period.

Squadron Leader Harris, who came from New Zealand but had a home in Birmingham where his wife lived, replaced S/L Wood as "B" Flight Commander – but he lasted barely three weeks in the role. On the 12th February, the Squadron took part in the near-suicidal daylight attack on the three German capital ships which had broken out of Brest in an attempt to reach open water. S/L Harris's PT-K failed to return: his body, and those of the two gunners, were later found and buried on the Dutch coast, but his navigator's body was never found. In a bad day for 420 Squadron, PT-J also disappeared without trace from the same mission: its pilot, P/O Topping, had joined 420 from 106 Squadron, with which he had won the DFM. The loss was claimed by night-fighters, but six Hampdens were claimed that day and it is not known for certain who fired the fatal shots.

Six nights later, and with operations to Mannheim and Cologne behind it, the Squadron lost another aircraft, when PT-F failed to return from a mine-laying mission. They found that the sea around the islands in the target area had frozen, making identification of individual islands difficult; and while they were re-orientating themselves, the searchlights, and then the tracer, got them. The aircraft was barely flying when it landed on the ice and slid, destroying itself. The pilot, F/O Kee (formerly of 44 Squadron), and his navigator, Sgt. Rutledge, survived due to the slightly nose-up attitude as it hit, but Sgt. Baker and Sgt. Adams in the rear of the aircraft took the full force of the impact, which killed them instantly. Someone, believed to be from the Dutch Resistance, found and released the pigeon, with a message written on the morning of 21st February giving a position - but not the true site of the crash - and the exhausted bird was found at Spurn Head in mid-afternoon the following day. The pigeon was awarded the Dickin

Medal (the "animal VC"), but the pilot and navigator were prisoners for the rest of the war.

Robert Rayne and his crew flew confidently with S/L Campbell in "A" Flight. The mission destinations mounted up: Wilhelmshaven, Kiel, together with smaller targets in Germany and the inevitable minelaying ("gardening" in Service parlance, due to the areas being coded by names of plants). Off-duty, they, like all the RAF personnel, found a warm welcome in Lincoln, as well as venturing further afield, to Nottingham and Grantham. Norman Axford had met a local Lincoln girl, a trainee teacher, and the relationship looked like becoming serious.

On March 3rd/4th, the CO led S/L Campbell and two other 420 Squadron aircraft (one flown by F/Sgt. Pinney[1]) to join forty-four other aircraft in a major raid on the Renault works at Billancourt near Paris. But for 44 Squadron, the date marked a most important event: the first-ever Lancaster raid, a minelaying operation led by Squadron Leader Nettleton. For both of the Waddington squadrons, it was a wholly satisfying and successful night – all eight aircraft returned safely, and the Hampden crews of 420 had virtually obliterated the factory they were sent to destroy.

Bomber Command visited Essen four times in the following weeks of March, as well as mounting a major offensive against Cologne. Seven Hampdens failed to return to their bases in this period, but 420 Squadron escaped this cull. The only problem, fortunately minor, occurred on 13th March when PT-

[1] *see page 42*

O got into difficulties due to icing: the pilot, F/Sgt. McDermid, told the crew "prepare to abandon aircraft", but the lower rear gunner, Sgt. Wilkinson, misunderstood the order and actually baled out, just as McDermid regained control of the aircraft. Fortunately, they were over England at the time, and Sgt. Wilkinson was soon back at Waddington, and continued to fly with the same crew, who obviously forgave him. (They had another lucky escape when they crashed in PT-P on return from Cologne at the end of May). The Squadron's luck ran out on March 27th, when PT-D was lost without trace from a minelaying operation, claimed by Ofw. Gildner of II/NFG2. The Sergeants' Mess lost four of its members, Sgt. Groff, the Canadian pilot, being accompanied in the aircraft by Sgt. Stalker, Sgt. Morgan (from Eckington in Derbyshire, the only Englishman in the otherwise Canadian crew) and Flight-Sergeant Williams. Two nights later, the third successive commander of "B" Flight went missing – S/L Tench and his crew in PT-V failed to return from a raid on Lübeck. Again, a nightfighter of II/NJG2 claimed responsibility, this time Uffz Merz. In the aftermath of this loss, other Squadron aircraft took off to look for the luckless Flight Commander, and one of them was attacked by a Spitfire on the way home. Even at that late stage of the Hampden's service, it seemed, Fighter Command too easily confused it with the German Heinkel or Dornier. ("If it's got two engines, it's German", in the reported words of one RAF fighter pilot who should have known better). Although this 420 Squadron aircraft crashed as a result, the crew survived and the aircraft was repaired, which was at least an improvement on the early days, when attacks on

Hampdens by Spitfires and Hurricanes led to losses of life and aircraft.

S/L Tench and his crew were all later reported as prisoners of war. S/L Forsythe took over the Flight, one Englishman replacing another in this nominally Canadian squadron.

Then at the end of March, W/Cdr Collier was posted to command 97 Squadron, and 420 received a Canadian CO, Wing Commander Bradshaw, who was accepted very quickly due to his evident concern that the Squadron should continue to work to the standards set by his predecessor. W/Cdr Bradshaw was great friends with W/Cdr Davoud, the commander of 409 (RCAF) Squadron and a fellow Canadian, and regularly visited Coleby Grange where the Beaufighters of 409 were stationed.

In the meantime, Flight-Sergeant John Timmis had completed his Bombing Leader's course in the second half of March, and shortly afterwards was commissioned, being gazetted on 17th April as Pilot Officer with the war-substantive rank of Flying Officer. For a few months he was therefore the senior ranking member of Zig-Zag's crew.

In the middle of April, 420 suffered the loss of three aircraft in as many days. First was F/Sgt. R. Johnson's PT-Y, lost without trace on a raid on Essen on the night of the 12th/13th April – possibly shot down by the night-fighter of Hauptman Lent, who claimed a Hampden in the Dutch Frisian Islands early on the morning of the 13th. Then came a big raid on Dortmund, scheduled for 14th/15th April, and a dreadful night for 420 Squadron. P/O Murray took off in PT-C to take part in the raid: it is believed he suffered a double engine failure immediately afterwards, and the Hampden crashed at North Hykeham barely three miles from Waddington. The bodies of the two gunners were returned to their home towns for burial; P/O Murray and his navigator P/O McCarthy – both Canadians - lie in the local churchyard in Waddington. And then F/Sgt. B. Johnson and his all-British crew in PT-G all lost their lives when the aircraft was shot down over Germany.

Five nights later, Sgt. Davis took his crew on a night training flight in PT-L, taking off at half-past midnight. Shortly afterwards, the aircraft crashed and burst into flames near Horncastle, and all on board were killed. Norman Axford, who had a Squadron photograph signed by many of those in the Sergeants' Mess (as well as P/O Rayne and S/L Campbell), gloomily marked off his friend Sgt. Laronde, the WOp/AG on PT-L, among the dead. The four members of the unlucky crew were buried near P/O Murray and P/O McCarthy at Waddington.

Dortmund was attacked again the following night, and there were major minelaying exercises on 19th/20th April and 22nd/23rd April. Then came the raids on Rostock, on three successive nights. 420 flew on the second raid, on the 24th/25th April, and PT-J went missing. It crashed in the early morning of the 25th on the Danish island of Fyn, killing the pilot, Sgt. Potter, and two of his crew: none of the three was over 21 years old. Only the lower rear gunner survived to be taken prisoner. Once again, II/NJG2 claimed victory, this time Lt. Linke.

Kiel, Paris and Hamburg all had visitations from the bombers in the next few nights.

"Zig-Zag"'s Aircrew & Ground crew. The "T" of the Squadron code can be seen to the left.

Sgt. J.H. Timmis, P/O R.N. Rayne, Sgt. N.F. Axford

Pilot, wireless-operator and navigator in relaxed poses

Norman Axford in his "Teddy-bear" flying suit.

The crew of Zig-Zag, like all the bomber crews, lived a strange dual existence: one night they would court death, flying straight and level through the flak to deliver their bomb load; the next, they might be enjoying the social life of Lincoln, seemingly a world away from the danger. Sgt. Axford was soon to propose to his girl, who was already wearing his "AG" sweetheart badge to signify her attachment to an RAF aircrew member.

May was an incident-packed month for 420 Squadron, and for Norman Axford. It began with a tale of great example of comradeship and courage in the face of danger. Sgt. Hiley RCAF, piloting PT-X, took part in a raid on Stuttgart, and on its way back to base the aircraft was hit by flak over Luxembourg. As if this was not enough, it was then attacked by a persistent Me. 110, which on its third attack, injured both Sgt. Hiley and the lower-rear airgunner, Sgt. Halward, the latter fatally. The WOp/AG, Sgt. Johnson (who with the navigator Sgt. Germain had signed Norman Axford's photograph), destroyed the night-fighter, but not before it had inflicted considerable damage, resulting in the loss of an engine and both compasses. The injured pilot managed to get it back as far as Essex, where it crash-landed near Colchester, and he was awarded an immediate DFM for his efforts. The body of Sgt. Halward, from Ontario, was buried at Ipswich.

On the same night, another 420 pilot earned his DFM: Sgt. Maitland came under flak attack as he crossed the coast on his outward flight, and was hit in the chest by one of the forty rounds which perforated the aircraft. With the port engine on fire, he abandoned the mission and brought the Hampden back to England, landing at Martlesham

Heath. The aircraft was repaired. (In December 1943, F/Lt. W.J.Maitland, DFM, RCAF – as he then was – was lost without trace on the first trip of his second tour of operations – to Berlin – flying a 408 Squadron Lancaster. He and his crew are all commemorated on the Runnymede Memorial).

Three days later, on May 8th, PT-D was lost on a minelaying mission. The pilot, Pilot Officer Carson, survived to be taken prisoner, but his three crew members lie buried in Kiel War Cemetery, among them the rear-gunner Sgt McDonnell, another of the signatories of Sgt. Axford's photo.

Then, on the next night, came a huge blow to "A" Flight when its commander, Squadron Leader Campbell went missing from a raid on Warnemünde. Four of the Lancasters from 44 Squadron were also lost in a terrible night for RAF Waddington, and indeed for Bomber Command, when the loss of twenty aircraft, from eleven different squadrons, meant that 116 telegrams were sent to next-of-kin regretting that their menfolk were missing. Of these, only 16 were taken prisoner-of-war; two of the sixteen were S/L Campbell and his rear-gunner, who survived when PT-A was hit by flak and crashed near Rostock. S/L Campbell (who found himself in Stalag Luft III at Sagan, along with S/L Wood and S/L Tench, the former leaders of "B" Flight, and three other 420 Squadron pilots) had at least had a comparatively good run in leading "A" Flight since its inception: "B" Flight had, in the same period, been commanded by four different men.

On May 20th, there was a nasty ground accident when a 44 Squadron Lancaster returning from a training flight swung on landing and collided with two of 420's parked Hampdens. PT-Q was written off (as was the Lancaster) and PT-B was damaged, but later repaired (following its service with 420, it went to Coastal Command and ended up with 32 OTU in Canada). Tragically, AC2 Commins, who had been working around the Hampdens, lost his life in the accident.

The following Saturday, Norman Axford's fiancée celebrated her 21st birthday, and it is believed that all the crew of Zig-Zag attended the party.

Then, at the end of the month, came Air Chief Marshall Harris's great plan – the first Thousand Bomber Raid, to Cologne. 420 Sqn, like all the others involved, mustered all available aircraft to take part in what was hoped would be a major blow to the German war effort – though in truth it was as much a do-or-die gamble by AOC Harris to prove to doubters that Bomber Command should remain as it was and not be split up, as the Army and Navy were both demanding. Although Sgt. Cybulski returned early due to problems with his aircraft (a repeat of his experience on the tragic Dortmund raid in April), for 420 the raid was a great success, with all crews returning safely, though F/Sgt. McDermid (who, with his entire crew, had signed Sgt. Axford's photograph), came back with battle damage and crashed on landing, writing-off PT-P and injuring himself and his navigator F/Sgt. Gardiner. In fact, 420 fared very well on the three "Thousand Bomber" raids, this being the only aircraft lost on them. Which was not to say that the period between Cologne and the final "Thousand" raid, to Bremen on 25th June, was not without its losses: PT-O went missing on a minelaying operation on 3rd June, and Sgts. Harrison, Gething, and Laing were all killed, only the W/Op, Sgt. Nall, surviving as a prisoner. Six days later, F/Sgt. Reid's entire crew of PT-N were killed when the aircraft was lost without trace on a raid to Essen, shot down by Hptm. Bunsch of III/NJG2 : thus N, O, and P were all lost within a ten-day period. The men who died in PT-N were very much a "Commonwealth" crew: the pilot and his wireless operator, Sgt. Copeland, were serving under the RCAF; the navigator, Sgt. Grabham, was with the Royal Australian Air Force, while the RAF Volunteer Reserve was represented by the lower rear gunner Sgt. Bunn.

On 17th June 1942, P/O Rayne's promotion to Flying Officer was gazetted, as was that of P/O Carson (exactly a year later, they were both promoted to Flight Lieutenant; Melville Carson and Robert Rayne had in fact followed parallel careers, both having been gazetted Pilot Officers (Probationary) on 17th June 1941).

The new PT-A did not last for long: the replacement for S/L Campbell's aircraft fell victim to a night-fighter on 21st June, on its way back from a raid on Emden. Once again, II/NJG2 was responsible, and again – as for PT-Y in April – Hptm. Lent claimed it. F/Sgt. Ellis and his crew – composed of RCAF, RAAF and RAFVR members in the same way as PT-N – all died. Another casualty that night was the lower gunner in F/Lt. Jacobs' Hampden: Sgt. Davidson RCAF, from Toronto, was mortally wounded on the return leg from an attack on Osnabruck, when the aircraft was fired on by a ship after they had crossed the Dutch coast. F/Lt. Jacobs got the Hampden back to Waddington, though he had to land it without wheels or flaps. Sgt. Davidson was buried at Waddington churchyard.

Two days later, Sgt. Hiley DFM, who had won his award at the beginning of May, took off in PT-L on a minelaying operation; twenty minutes later, the aircraft came down near Grantham, injuring the pilot and killing the rest of the crew. Norman Axford marked up two more losses on his photograph: F/Sgt. Germain, the navigator, and Sgt. Johnson, the W/Op, were both on board. Both Sgt. Germain and F/Sgt. Little, the lower gunner, hailed from Ontario, from Newmarket and Lambeth respectively.

The third of July saw the loss of the third PT-A in two months (and the second successive one to fall to II/NJG2) when F/Lt. Brown was caught by Oblt. Prinz zur Lippe-Weisenfeld on the way back from Bremen (the Thousand Bomber "follow-up" raid), and crashed in Holland. The pilot escaped, to be taken prisoner, but his crew died, including Sgt. Waddington, the W/Op who had survived the crash of PT-P after the Thousand Bomber raid and who was another of Norman Axford's signatories. Another night-fighter from the same Luftwaffe squadron, Fw. Grimm, claimed PT-T less than an hour later, and F/Sgt. Wilde and all his crew died. At 33, the wireless operator in this crew, F/Sgt. Crothers, from Cooksville, Ontario, was possibly the oldest aircrew member killed in action with the 420 Hampdens: by contrast, the lower gunner, Jack Gibbs, also from Ontario, was only 19 and was probably the youngest. He had added five years to his age to get into the RCAF.

A short rest, and the Hampdens went back to Wilhelmshaven on July 8th/9th. Three days later, PT-Z was shot down during a minelaying operation, with the loss of Sgt. Hannah RCAF and his crew.

The bodies of the pilot and his W/Op, F/Sgt. Bull DFM, were never found, and they are commemorated on the Runnymede Memorial. F/Sgt. Bull had won his medal in September 1941, while a Sergeant with 44 Squadron.

Duisburg received the bombers' attention next, and then came another major raid on Hamburg, on the night of 26th/27th July. Fifteen Hampdens from 420 Squadron joined eighteen from 408; Robert Rayne and his crew were flying AE202, PT-K, that night. The lower rear gunner on this trip was Sgt. Elliott. Of the fifteen aircraft from 420 Squadron which took off, four returned early, and the remaining eleven fought their way to the target through heavy cloud and icing conditions. But the searchlights around Hamburg were busy, and so were the night-fighters. One 408 crew found themselves being attacked shortly after their bombing run, but managed to escape into cloud.

PT-K also completed its bombing run successfully, and headed for home. Just as P/O Timmis announced that he could see the coast ahead, Norman Axford warned Robert Rayne that a fighter was coming up. The pilot took immediate evasive action, and tracer streamed over his head as he turned, the aircraft passing quickly in and out of the stream. Feeling the Hampden shudder, he hurriedly checked all of his crew, and each answered that they were all right. But a second later the fighter attacked again, and the Hampden was enveloped in flames. Giving the order to bale out, Robert Rayne found that he couldn't release his harness: thankfully, he soon managed to free himself and as he floated down by parachute he heard the sea below him, but in fact he landed on the sand. His crew were not so lucky: they all died with the Hampden, and were buried in the local churchyard at Tönning: at the end of the war they were transferred to Kiel War Cemetery. The crew of Zig-Zag, all of them RAF Volunteer Reserve, were no more.

To compound the misery for 420, F/Sgt. Johnstone's PT-V disappeared from the same mission, and was presumed lost at sea. The wireless operator, Pilot Officer Tilling, was a regular RAF officer, the rest of the crew being RCAF.

The last night of July saw a trip to Dusseldorf, and yet another aircraft was lost without trace, when W/O Kaufman and his crew in PT-A failed to return. This, too, was almost entirely an RCAF crew, only the lower rear gunner being RAF Volunteer Reserve.

That was the not only the last Hampden lost from service with 420 Squadron; it was also the squadron's last Hampden mission, and indeed the last time 420 Squadron flew with Lincolnshire's 5 Group. On 7th August, the "Snowy Owl" Squadron moved to Skipton-on-Swale in Yorkshire, to fly Wellingtons with 4 Group, which was collecting all the Canadian squadrons together. In just short of eight months flying Hampdens, 420 had carried out 535 sorties, covering 44 bombing raids, 37 minelaying missions, 8 leaflet raids and one weather reconnaissance flight. It had lost 24 aircraft on operations, plus one in training and one in a ground collision. Seventy-six aircrew had lost their lives, with a further seventeen taken prisoner-of-war, and one ground-crew member had been killed in the collision at dispersal.

AFTERMATH

Robert Rayne ended up in Stalag Luft 3 at Sagan, alongside his Flight Commander S/L Campbell and the other officer prisoners-of-war from 420 Squadron. There, he was among those sending coded messages to IS9, giving such military information as came their way. In this, he was joined by S/L Campbell, F/Lt. Carson and S/L Tench, as well, of course, as many others. (Prominent on the list is S/L Roger Bushell, who led "the Great Escape" from the camp and was one of the 50 escapers shot by the Gestapo).

Flying Officer Robert Needell Rayne of 420 Squadron was awarded the Distinguished Flying Cross in early 1943, five months after S/L Graham Campbell received the same award. As both were in Stalag Luft 3 at the times of their gazetting, the investitures were presumably somewhat delayed!

Following his return to the UK, Flight-Lieutenant Robert Rayne, DFC was appointed second-in-command to Colonel Alan Andrews of the Army Education Corps. On demobilisation, he returned to academia, teaching at Manchester Grammar School before becoming a lecturer in Classics, and Men's Warden, of the University College of North Staffordshire (later Keele University), where he was remembered by one student as being "of soft voice but eagle eye – apparently able to see entirely through the intentions of any teenager within 30 yards". He left Keele in 1963 with his wife and family to become Vice-President of the Chung Chi College, part of the University of Hong Kong, rising to President of the College in 1975/76, before returning to Oxfordshire on retirement. He died at the turn of the millennium.

Another inmate of Stalag Luft 3 was Robert Kee, the pilot of the luckless PT-F – who was, like Robert Rayne, an Oxford graduate – and following his return to the UK, he entered the world of the media and became a well-known (and BAFTA-winning) television presenter as well as a successful author.

Norman Axford's fiancée retained a small spark of hope that he had somehow survived, a spark she kept alive for nearly three years and which was only finally extinguished when Robert Rayne returned to confirm that his crew had all died. She later married and had children, but kept in touch with the Axford family.

420 Squadron, RCAF, only stayed at Skipton-on-Swale for two months before moving to Middleton St. George, Durham. It became a founder-member of the Canadian 6 Group in January 1943 and was detached to the Middle East between May and November 1943. On its return, it was equipped with Handley-Page Halifax bombers and based at Tolthorpe, Yorkshire, and shared in the grievous losses suffered by Bomber Command in 1944. Disbanded after the war, it has become one of the "forgotten" squadrons, with very little detailed history available. The "Hampden" period is particularly neglected, some records only recognising 420 Squadron when it became part of No 6 (RCAF) Group.

WHICH AIRCRAFT WAS "ZIG-ZAG"?

The identity of the aircraft which "belonged" to Robert Rayne and his crew is very difficult to ascertain. None of the photographs known to exist show the registration number, nor even the Squadron identity letter – in one photograph, the "T" of the "PT" code can be seen, but the crew (whether by accident or design) are hiding the aircraft letter and the registration number, which was painted on the fuselage immediately ahead of the tail. It is quite possible that the war-time censor would have insisted that all identification was removed, though this does not seem to have been an issue with other photographs of wartime aircraft; and hence it is more likely that it is simply an unfortunate coincidence that personnel continually hid the codes.

It seems, however, unlikely that "Zig-Zag" was AE202, the aircraft in which P/O Timmis, Sgt. Axford and Sgt. Elliott met their deaths. AE202 was a veteran of 44 Squadron, and one of the most-photographed of all Hampdens when it formed part of a flight of three 44 Squadron aircraft sent aloft for the benefit of the press, for RAF publicity purposes. Then coded KM-K, it was in company with KM-X (AE257) and KM-A (AD981) – both of which were also lost on operations, AE257 on the night of 21st/22nd October 1941 on a mission to Bremen, and AD981 when it ran out of fuel coming back from Rostock on 12th September 1941 and ditched off Cromer, its crew being rescued by HMS *Garth*. AE202 soldiered on with 44 Squadron until the fateful day of 13th December 1941, when it was flown by S/L Burton-Gyles DFC (then S/L Wood's Flight Commander) on the minelaying mission which claimed the life of W/Cdr Misselbrook. AE202 was attacked by Messerschmitt Bf109s and sustained considerable damage, losing the starboard wingtip, starboard rudder, and starboard engine fairing and nacelle. Perhaps needless to add, the starboard engine was damaged, as was the starboard aileron, mainplane and airscrew, and the starboard undercarriage was hit and the tyre punctured. Burton-Gyles not only got the aircraft home but landed it safely. But it would hardly be in a fit state to be handed over to 420 Squadron in January, and indeed the assumption has to be that it was not. It served 420 as PT-K, which implies that its identity was changed by simply painting out the "KM" codes and replacing them with "PT" – but 420 had another PT-K, AT134, which was S/L Harris's aircraft when he led "B" Flight, and was lost on 12th February. AT134 was, like S/L Wood's PT-S (AT130), a relatively new Hampden, and it seems likely that it was taken on strength by 44 Squadron at the time when AE202 was being repaired, and hence was issued with the KM-K code which was later changed to PT-K. AE202 presumably returned from repair subsequent to 12th February, and also kept its "K" code, with the "KM" Squadron marking again being replaced by "PT". The alternative, that AE202 was issued with a different identity letter and was then re-assigned the "K" identity when AT134 was lost, scarcely seems credible – it is unlikely that anyone would decide to make such a change out of sentiment.

[It should be noted that some sources record AE202 as "PT-X". It is believed this stems from a mis-reading of the Squadron loss-record card, which is admittedly rather poorly written, but it certainly looks more like a "K" than an "X". The loss record card (possibly completed after Robert Rayne's repatriation) also shows the crews' ranks as pilot, F/Lt Rayne, navigator P/O Timmis - though the same sources which quote "PT-X" also tend, incorrectly, to show the ranks as P/O and Sergeant respectively. In the latter case at least, the error would seem to have been perpetrated by the Air Ministry which quoted the rank of F/Sgt. in the communiqué detailing casualties].

If it is further assumed that Robert Rayne's crew had already been allocated "Zig-Zag" before the middle of February (as also seems likely), it follows that this could not be AE202.

It may be that the name followed from its identity letter, and that "Zig-Zag" was indeed PT-Z. That aircraft, AE390, was, of course, lost on 13th July when F/Sgt. Hannah took it minelaying and did not return. This could well have been the reason why Robert Rayne's crew took AE202 on their final mission a fortnight later – if their "personal" aircraft had already been lost, they would of course need an alternative.

Sadly, all of this is mere speculation. Unless there are some further photographs which identify the particular machine, or any of the ex-Squadron members (should any be still around) can remember, it seems destined to remain one of those issues which is unlikely to be resolved.

420 (SNOWY OWL) SQUADRON RCAF

In Memory of the Hampden Aircrew and Groundcrew who died in action and in aircraft losses

		Age		Aircraft	Burial*
ADAMS, James Richard Branston	Sergeant,RAFVR (AG)	24	18-Feb-42	AD915	Schiermonnikoog(Vyrenhoef)
ASHFIELD, Frederick William	Sergeant,RAFVR (Navigator)	n/k	12-Feb-42	P4400	Runnymede
AXFORD, Norman Frank	Sergeant,RAFVR (WOp/AG)	20	27-Jul-42	AE202	Kiel
BAKER, Horace	Sergeant,RAFVR (WOp/AG)	22	18-Feb-42	AD915	Schiermonnikoog(Vyrenhoef)
BIRCH, Kenneth Alan	Sergeant,RAFVR (AG)	22	14-Apr-42	AT219	Yardley Wood
BLACK, Robert Hammond	Flight-Sergeant,RAFVR (WOp/AG)	22	13-Apr-42	P1239	Runnymede
BOND, Alan Dennis	Sergeant,RAFVR (Navigator)	30	03-Jul-42	P5332	Vollenhove
BRUNT, Arthur Havelock	Flight-Sergeant,RAF (WOp/AG)	20	12-Feb-42	AT134	The Hague
BULL, Peter Ernest, DFM	Flight-Sergeant,RAFVR (WOp/AG)	22	13-Jul-42	AE390	Runnymede
BUNN, Cecil James	Sergeant,RAFVR (AG)	22	08-Jun-42	AT136	Runnymede
BUTLER, Cyril John Edmund	Sergeant,RAFVR (Navigator)	n/k	13-Apr-42	P1239	Runnymede
CHAPMAN, William John	Sergeant,RAFVR (Navigator)	n/k	13-Jul-42	AE390	Lorient
COMMINS, Oliver Frederick	AC2,RAFVR (Ground)	33	20-May-42	P2094	Exeter Higher
COPELAND, Herbert Redvers	Sergeant,RCAF (WOp/AG)	28	08-Jun-42	AT136	Runnymede
CROTHERS, Thomas Edward	Flight-Sergeant,RCAF (WOp/AG)	33	03-Jul-42	P5332	Amersfoort
DAVIS, Hershel Homer	Sergeant,RCAF (Pilot)	n/k	19-Apr-42	AD869	Waddington
DAVIDSON, Roy	Sergeant, RCAF (WOp/AG)	25	21-Jun-42	AE401	Waddington
ELLIOTT, John Ridley	Sergeant,RAFVR (AG)	n/k	27-Jul-42	AE202	Kiel
ELLIS, George Henry	Flight-Sergeant,RCAF (Pilot)	28	21-Jun-42	AT185	Ameland (NES)
FOWLER, Edward Graham	Flying Officer,RAFVR (WOp/AG)	30	12-Feb-42	P4400	Runnymede
FROST, William David	Pilot Officer,RCAF (WOp/AG)	24	01-Aug-42	AE355	Runnymede
GERMAIN, George Henry	Flight-Sergeant,RCAF (Navigator)	28	23-Jun-42	AD786	Lincoln Newport
GETHING, James Steele	Sergeant,RAFVR (Navigator)	n/k	03-Jun-42	AE260	Guidel
GIBBS, Jack Edward	Flight-Sergeant,RCAF (AG)	19	03-Jul-42	P5332	Vollenhove
GRABHAM, Arthur James	Sergeant,RAAF (Navigator)	20	08-Jun-42	AT136	Runnymede
GREENAWAY, Arthur John	Sergeant,RAFVR (AG)	22	01-Aug-42	AE355	Runnymede
GROFF, Wilfred Rodgers	Sergeant,RCAF (Pilot)	23	26-Mar-42	AE298	Runnymede

Name	Rank	Age	Date	Serial	Location
HALWARD, James Frederick (Jim)	Flight-Sergeant,RCAF (AG)	23	05-May-42	P1187	Ipswich
HANNAH, Thomas John	Flight-Sergeant,RCAF (Pilot)	21	13-Jul-42	AE390	Runnymede
HARRIS, George Taylor Bernays	Squadron Leader,RAF (Pilot)	28	12-Feb-42	AT134	Amsterdam New Eastern
HARRISON, Ernest	Sergeant,RAFVR (Pilot)	21	03-Jun-42	AE260	Guidel
HICKS, Joseph Melvin	Sergeant,RCAF (Navigator)	21	25-Apr-42	P5330	Assens (FYN)
JOHNSON, Ronald	Flight-Sergeant,RAFVR (Pilot)	26	13-Apr-42	P1239	Runnymede
JOHNSON, Bradley Winship	Flight-Sergeant,RAFVR (Pilot)	27	15-Apr-42	AT218	Rheinberg
JOHNSON, George Debbage	Sergeant,RAFVR (WOp/AG)	26	23-Jun-42	AD786	Walthamstow (St Marys)
JOHNSON, Keith Alan	Flight-Sergeant,RAFVR (WOp/AG)	22	14-Apr-42	AT219	Fordham (SS Peter & Mary Magdalene)
JOHNSTONE, Alan Taylor	Flight-Sergeant,RCAF (Pilot)	20	27-Jul-42	AE267	Runnymede
KAUFMAN, William John	W/Officer 2,RCAF (Pilot)	23	01-Aug-42	AE355	Runnymede
LAING, Gerard Joseph	Sergeant,RAFVR (AG)	21	03-Jun-42	AE260	Guidel
LARONDE, Gerald Greville Joseph	Flight-Sergeant,RCAF (WOp/AG)	21	19-Apr-42	AD869	Waddington
LAW, Harold Naismith	W/Officer 2,RCAF (Navigator)	24	27-Jul-42	AE267	Runnymede
LITTLE, Kingsley Clarence	Flight-Sergeant,RCAF (AG)	31	23-Jun-42	AD786	Lincoln Newport
MATE, Thomas Henry	Sergeant,RAFVR (AG)	n/k	12-Feb-42	P4400	Runnymede
McCARTHY, William Francis	Pilot Officer,RCAF (Navigator)	22	14-Apr-42	AT219	Waddington
McDONNELL, William Albert	Sergeant,RAFVR (AG)	26	08-May-42	AE389	Kiel
McHARDY, John Charles Donald	Sergeant,RAFVR (AG)	25	15-Apr-42	AT218	Rheinberg
MILLER, Hubert Harvey	Flying Officer,RCAF (Navigator)	31	12-Feb-42	AT134	Runnymede
MORGAN, Rhedge Haydn Durham	Sergeant,RAFVR (WOp/AG)	n/k	26-Mar-42	AE298	Runnymede
MURRAY, William James	Pilot Officer,RCAF (Pilot)	20	14-Apr-42	AT219	Waddington
NIDELMAN, Bernard Davis	Flight-Sergeant,RCAF (WOp/AG)	21	21-Jun-42	AT185	Runnymede
PARRY, Ronald Robert	Sergeant,RAFVR (WOp/AG)	21	09-May-42	AT144	Berlin 1939-1945
PETERSEN, Reginald Bruce	Flight-Sergeant,RCAF (Navigator)	n/k	09-May-42	AT144	Berlin 1939-1945
PLAYER, Geoffrey Albert	Sergeant,RAFVR (AG)	n/k	19-Apr-42	AD869	Waddington
POTTER, Jack	Sergeant,RAFVR (Pilot)	21	25-Apr-42	P5330	Assens (FYN)
PRICE, John James	Flight-Sergeant,RCAF (AG)	23	27-Jul-42	AE267	Runnymede
PRITCHARD, Joseph Corbin	Flight-Sergeant,RCAF (Navigator)	25	19-Apr-42	AD869	Waddington

Name	Rank	Age	Date	Aircraft	Location
REID, Ian McLaren	Flight-Sergeant, RCAF (Pilot)	24	08-Jun-42	AT136	Runnymede
ROTHERY, Percy Vernon Edward	Sergeant, RAFVR (AG)	21	12-Feb-42	AT134	The Hague
SALMON, Japhet	Sergeant, RAFVR (AG)	n/k	13-Apr-42	P1239	Runnymede
SHIPTON, Joseph Preston	Sergeant, RAFVR (WOp/AG)	24	15-Apr-42	AT218	Rheinberg
SMITH, James Henry	Flight-Sergeant, RCAF (WOp/AG)	20	25-Apr-42	P5330	Assens (FYN)
STALKER, Leonard Ogilvy	Sergeant, RCAF (Navigator)	23	26-Mar-42	AE298	Runnymede
STEWART, Robert Reginald	W/Officer 2, RCAF (Navigator)	n/k	01-Aug-42	AE355	Runnymede
STILL, Leonard George	Sergeant, RAFVR (AG)	21	21-Jun-42	AT185	Runnymede
THOMSON, James Anderson	Flight-Sergeant, RCAF (AG)	n/k	13-Jul-42	AE390	Lorient
TILLING, George Edward	Pilot Officer, RAF (WOp/AG)	n/k	27-Jul-42	AE267	Runnymede
TIMMIS, John Harold (Jack)	Pilot Officer, RAFVR (Navigator)	28	27-Jul-42	AE202	Kiel
TOPPING, John Robert, DFM	Pilot Officer, RAFVR (Pilot)	24	12-Feb-42	P4400	Runnymede
URQUHART, Alexander Scouler	Sergeant, RAFVR (WOp/AG)	n/k	08-May-42	AE389	Kiel
VOSPER, Henry Ernest	Sergeant, RAFVR (Navigator)	21	15-Apr-42	AT218	Rheinberg
WADDELL, Hilton Graham	Pilot Officer, RAAF (Navigator)	22	21-Jun-42	AT185	Sage
WADDINGTON, John Noel	Sergeant, RAFVR (WOp/AG)	22	03-Jul-42	AE248	Hemelumer Oldeferd
WHYTOCK, Robert William	Sergeant, RAFVR (AG)	n/k	03-Jul-42	AE248	Hemelumer Oldeferd
WILDE, Charles Garnett	Flight-Sergeant, RCAF (Pilot)	22	03-Jul-42	P5332	Amersfoort
WILLIAMS, Arthur Frederick	Flight-Sergeant, RCAF (AG)	27	26-Mar-42	AE298	Runnymede
WILLIAMS, Graham Colin	Sergeant, RAFVR (Navigator)	28	08-May-42	AE389	Kiel
WILLIAMS, Robert Oscar	Sergeant, RAFVR (Navigator)	24	03-Jul-42	AE248	Hemelumer Oldeferd

* "Runnymede" means the Runnymede Memorial to those aircrew who have no known grave. These are mainly believed to be lost over sea. Many of these men would have been classified WOp/AG.

Note: "AG" identifies the lower rear gunner of the relevant aircraft.

420 (SNOWY OWL) SQUADRON RCAF

Hampden Aircrew Prisoners-of-War

			Aircraft	Camp
ADAMS, F G W	W/Officer 2 (AG)	25-Apr-42	P5330	Stalag Kopernikus
BOTT, R L	Sergeant (AG)	21-Jan-42	AT130	Stalag Hohen Fels
BROWN, K E	Flight-Lieutenant (Pilot)	03-Jul-42	AE248	Stalag Luft 3 Sagan
CAMPBELL, G C	Squadron Leader (Pilot)	09-May-42	AT144	Stalag Luft 3 Sagan
CARSON, M F	Flight-Lieutenant (Pilot)	08-May-42	AE389	Stalag Luft 3 Sagan
DURNAM, F A	Sergeant (AG)	29-Mar-42	AE246	Stalag Lamsdorf
GREALY, D de L	Warrant Officer (Navigator)	21-Jan-42	AT130	Stalag Luft Heydekrug
HYDE, K T	W/Officer 2 (Navigator)	29-Mar-42	AE246	Stalag Lamsdorf
KEE, R L	Flight-Lieutenant (Pilot)	18-Feb-42	AD915	Stalag Luft 3 Sagan
NALL, L C	Sergeant (WOp/AG)	03-Jun-42	AE260	Stalag Kopernikus
RAYNE, R N	Flight-Lieutenant (Pilot)	27-Jul-42	AE202	Stalag Luft 3 Sagan
RUTLEDGE, W H J	Sergeant (Navigator)	18-Feb-42	AD915	Stalag Lamsdorf
SEMPLE, D G	Sergeant (WOp/AG)	21-Jan-42	AT130	Stalag Hohen Fels
SOPER, G H	Flight-Lieutenant (AG)	09-May-42	AT144	Stalag Luft 3 Sagan
TENCH, G R	Squadron Leader (Pilot)	29-Mar-42	AE246	Stalag Luft 3 Sagan
THORNE, H	Warrant Officer (WOp/AG)	29-Mar-42	AE246	Stalag Luft 3 Sagan
WOOD, V T L	Squadron Leader (Pilot)	21-Jan-42	AT130	Stalag Luft 3 Sagan

CITATIONS

Among the medals awarded to those who were, or had been, Hampden aircrew of 420 squadron were the following:-

Distinguished Flying Cross

BISHOP, F/Lt. **Joseph William**, AG: Gazetted 11th June 1943. The main action specified in the citation was the feat of shooting out three searchlights in quick succession, enabling his aircraft (which had been coned by them) to escape. The date of the award (and the fact that he was able to do this!) suggests that this happened in the post-Hampden period, probably when 420 was operating the Wellington with 4 Group. (*see also page 50*)

CAMPBELL, S/L **Graham Cox**, Pilot: Gazetted 20th November 1942. The citation spoke of his great courage and resourcefulness, and that he "sets a splendid example". Although Canadian, he initially served in the RAF, transferring to the RCAF in 1944 while still in captivity (he was not alone in doing so, although the mechanism enabling this is obscure). He returned to the UK in May 1945, and to Canada in September of that year. He retired from the RCAF in 1961 and died in 1998. (*see also text*).

CYBULSKI, P/O **Stanley Julian**, Pilot: Gazetted 22nd September 1942. P/O Cybulski (commissioned in June 1942), aged 23, took part in 24 operations between 22nd February and 14th July 1942 (when the award was recommended), although he was forced to return early from four of them. On another occasion, he turned back when an engine failed shortly after crossing the English coast, but got it running again after twenty minutes, on which he turned again and completed the mission. The citation said that he "maintained a very high standard as a bomber captain and has set an excellent example to the remainder of the squadron". He was invested by King George VI two weeks before his death (*see also page 49*).

DART, (Acting)F/Lt. **Adrian Peter**. Pilot: Gazetted 4th August 1942. The citations spoke of the number of sorties he had flown, stating that he was "a skilful pilot held in high esteem by all aircrew of the squadron". Five months after receiving the DFC, and as a Squadron-Leader with 419(RCAF) Squadron, he was gazetted DSO.

GARDINER, W/O **Llewellyn Hugh Cloverdale**, Navigator: Gazetted 20th April 1943. Aged 26, his citation declared him to have "set a high standard of navigational skill and devotion to duty". (*See also page 49*).

HYNAM, P/O **Graham Stanley**, Pilot: Gazetted 8th January 1943. The citation noted that in his attacks on "the enemy's most heavily defended targets, [he] has achieved success with almost unfailing regularity [and] the greatest resolve and spirit". From Akron, Ohio, he was flying a 23 OTU Wellington in a "Wings for Victory" flypast over Pershore on 29th May 1943 when a wing broke off. Along with the rest of the crew, and two civilians on the ground, he was killed, aged 23.

JACOBS, (Acting) S/L **David Sinclair**, Pilot: Gazetted 20th April 1943. The citation noted that he had flown to Italy with the aircraft "virtually undefended" when the rear turret became unserviceable over France; he had also flown through 40 minutes of intense anti-aircraft fire en route to Hamburg. His determination to succeed was noted. Later promoted to Wing-Commander, he was Officer Commanding 408 Squadron, RCAF when his Lancaster was shot down by a night-fighter during a mission to Dortmund on 22nd May 1944, and all on board were killed. He was a graduate of McGill University in Toronto, and his wife lived in that city. (*see also page 26*).

KIRBY, P/O **Herbert Harry**, Navigator: Gazetted 12th January 1943. Awarded for "numerous sorties including attacks on targets in the heavily-defended Ruhr area as well as at Rostock and Lubeck ... also...several mine-laying sorties." Survived tour of operations, promoted Flying Officer, killed while serving with 19 OTU, 14th August 1943.

MANN, P/O **Lloyd Robertson**, WOp/AG: Gazetted 12th January 1943. Aged 23, he was a member of Stanley Cybulski's crew and, like his captain, was commissioned in June 1942. His citation spoke of him having, "on several occasions and by his technical skill, enabled his captain to fly a badly damaged aircraft safely to base... his cheerfulness and devotion to duty under the most trying conditions have set a high example to his crew." Promoted to F/O, he transferred from 420 to 156 Squadron with Stanley Cybulski, and they died together in December 1942.

PINNEY, W/O **Edward Frank William**, Pilot: Gazetted 4th August 1942. His citation spoke of his splendid example to less experienced crews. Later commissioned (gazetted as Flight Lieutenant, January 1945). As his name cannot be found in either the casualty or PoW records, it would seem he survived the war.

RAYNE, F/O **Robert Needell**, Pilot: Gazetted 20th April 1943. The citation spoke of the number of successful sorties carried out, including Essen, Cologne, Bremen, Duisberg and Rostock, and noted that he took part in the attacks on the capital ships in Brest. From the wording, it would seem more likely that the latter was the sortie on 31st January/1st February 1942, rather than the "Channel Dash" of 12th February. (*see text*)

WAYLAND, P/O **John Albert Meredith**, W/Op: Gazetted 29th December 1942. The citation spoke of the many sorties he had undertaken over heavily-defended targets, with specific mention of his taking part in an attack on the *Gneisenau*.

Distinguished Flying Medal

ARMSTRONG, F/Sgt. **Robert**, Navigator: Gazetted 14th April 1942. The citation listed a number of major targets, and said that several of these sorties had been "carried out under difficult conditions" (*sic.*).

CHAMPION, Sgt. **Frederick John Joseph**, WOp/AG: Gazetted 29th December 1942, the citation noting that he had participated in numerous sorties including those against heavily-defended targets. (*see page 50*).

HILEY, Sgt. **Frederick Staples**, Pilot: Gazetted 29th May 1942 (*see page 23*)

HOOKER, F/Sgt. **Ernest Leslie**, WOp/AG: Gazetted 29th December 1942. The citation spoke of his long and outstanding career in which he had never experienced a failure with his wireless equipment. Later commissioned, he had reached the rank of F/O when he was killed on 20th September 1944, on a training flight in the Lancaster captained by F/O Hogg (training leader) whose aircraft was in collision with another Lancaster when they entered cloud during formation flying practice.

MAITLAND, Sgt. **William John**, Pilot: Gazetted 29th May 1942 (*see page 23*)

TRENDELL, Sgt. **Edward Lawrence**, WOp: Gazetted 29th December 1942. The citation regarded him as a highly reliable wireless-operator, but the main reason for the award would seem to be that he had been largely responsible for enabling his wounded captain to fly back to the UK, one engine having been set on fire. As with F/Lt Bishop, above, the classification (WOp instead of WOp/AG) would seem to indicate the post-Hampden period of this event. (*see also page 49*)

(From the above list, it would appear that 29th December 1942 was the date on which the efforts of a number of wireless operators were recognised).

420 (RCAF) SQUADRON ROYAL AIR FORCE

HAMPDEN LOSSES
(Note: "(K)" means Killed; "(P)" means taken Prisoner-of-War)

21-Jan-42	AT130 PT-S	Emden	S/L V T L WOOD (Pilot)	(P)
			Sgt D de L GREALY (Navigator)	(P)
			Sgt D G SEMPLE (WOp/AG)	(P)
			Sgt R L BOTT (AG)	(P)
12-Feb-42	P4400 PT-J	Fuller	P/O J R TOPPING DFM (Pilot)	(K)
			Sgt F W ASHFIELD (Nav.)	(K)
			F/O E G FOWLER (WOp/AG)	(K)
			Sgt T H MATE (AG)	(K)
12-Feb-42	AT134 PT-K	Fuller	S/L G L B HARRIS (Pilot)	(K)
			F/O H H MILLER (Navigator)	(K)
			F/S A H BRUNT (WOp/AG)	(K)
			Sgt P V E ROTHERY (AG)	(K)
18-Feb-42	AD915 PT-F	Minelaying	F/O R KEE (Pilot)	(P)
			Sgt W H J RUTLEDGE (Nav.)	(P)
			Sgt H BAKER (WOp/AG)	(K)
			Sgt J R B ADAMS (AG)	(K)
26-Mar-42	AE298 PT-D	Minelaying	Sgt W R GROFF (Pilot)	(K)
			Sgt L O STALKER (Nav.)	(K)
			Sgt R H D MORGAN (WOp/AG)	(K)
			F/S A F WILLIAMS (AG)	(K)
29-Mar-42	AE246 PT-V	Lubeck	S/L G R TENCH (Pilot)	(P)
			Sgt K T HYDE (Nav.)	(P)
			F/S H THORNE (WOp/AG)	(P)
			Sgt F A DURNAM (AG)	(P)
13-Apr-42	P1239 PT-Y	Essen	F/S R JOHNSON (Pilot)	(K)
			Sgt C J E BUTLER (Nav.)	(K)
			F/S R H BLACK (WOp/AG)	(K)
			Sgt J SALMON (AG)	(K)
14-Apr-42	AT219 PT-C	Dortmund	P/O W J MURRAY (Pilot)	(K)
			P/O W F E McCARTHY (Nav.)	(K)
			F/S K A JOHNSON (WOp/AG)	(K)
			Sgt K A BIRCH (AG)	(K)

15-Apr-42	AT218 PT-G	Dortmund	F/S B W JOHNSON (Pilot)	(K)
			Sgt H E VOSPER (Navigator)	(K)
			Sgt J P SHIPTON (WOp/AG)	(K)
			Sgt J C D McHARDY (AG)	(K)
19-Apr-42	AD869 PT-L	Training	Sgt H H DAVIS (Pilot)	(K)
			F/S J C PRITCHARD (Nav.)	(K)
			F/S G G J LARONDE (W/AG)	(K)
			Sgt G C PLAYER (AG)	(K)
25-Apr-42	P5330 PT-J	Rostock	Sgt J POTTER (Pilot)	(K)
			Sgt J M HICKS (Navigator)	(K)
			F/S J H SMITH (WOp/AG)	(K)
			Sgt F G W ADAMS (AG)	(P)
05-May-42	P1187 PT-X	Stuttgart	Sgt F S HILEY (Pilot)	
			Sgt G H GERMAIN (Nav.)	
			Sgt G D JOHNSON (WOp/AG)	
			F/S J F HALWARD (AG)	(K)
08-May-42	AE389 PT-D	Minelaying	P/O M F CARSON (Pilot)	(P)
			Sgt G C WILLIAMS (Nav.)	(K)
			Sgt A S URQUHART (W/AG)	(K)
			Sgt W A McDONNELL (AG)	(K)
09-May-42	AT144 PT-A	Warnemunde	S/L G C CAMPBELL (Pilot)	(P)
			F/S R B PETERSEN (Nav.)	(K)
			Sgt R R PARRY (WOp/AG)	(K)
			Sgt G H SOPER (AG)	(P)
20-May-42	P2094 PT-Q	Ground	AC2 O F COMMINS	(K)
31-May-42	AE399 PT-P	Köln	F/S W K McDERMID (Pilot)	
			F/S L H GARDINER (Nav.)	
			Sgt J N WADDINGTON (W/AG)	
			Sgt. R G WILKINSON (AG)	
03-Jun-42	AE260 PT-O	Minelaying	Sgt E HARRISON (Pilot)	(K)
			Sgt J S GETHING (Nav.)	(K)
			Sgt L C NALL (WOp/AG)	(P)
			Sgt G J LAING (AG)	(K)

Date	Aircraft	Target	Crew	
08-Jun-42	AT136 PT-N	Essen	F/S I M REID (Pilot)	(K)
			Sgt A J GRABHAM (Nav.)	(K)
			Sgt H R COPELAND (W/AG)	(K)
			Sgt C J BUNN (AG)	(K)
21-Jun-4	AT185 PT-A	Emden	F/S G H ELLIS (Pilot)	(K)
			P/O H G WADDELL (Nav.)	(K)
			F/S B D NIDELMAN (WOp/AG)	(K)
			Sgt L G STILL (AG)	(K)
23-Jun-42	AD786 PT-L	Minelaying	Sgt F S HILEY DFM (Pilot)	
			F/S G H GERMAIN (Nav.)	(K)
			Sgt G D JOHNSON (WOp/AG)	(K)
			F/S K C LITTLE (AG)	(K)
03-Jul-42	P5332 PT-T	Bremen	F/S C G WILDE (Pilot)	(K)
			Sgt A D BOND (Navigator)	(K)
			F/S T E CROTHERS (W/AG)	(K)
			F/S J E GIBBS (AG)	(K)
03-Jul-42	AE248 PT-A	Bremen	F/Lt K E BROWN (Pilot)	(P)
			Sgt R O WILLIAMS (Nav.)	(K)
			Sgt J N WADDINGTON (W/AG)	(K)
			F/S R W WHYTOCK (AG)	(K)
13-Jul-42	AE390 PT-Z	Minelaying	F/S T J HANNAH (Pilot)	(K)
			Sgt W J CHAPMAN (Nav.)	(K)
			F/S P E BULL, DFM (W/AG)	(K)
			F/S J A THOMSON (AG)	(K)
27-Jul-42	AE202 PT-K	Hamburg	F/O R N RAYNE (Pilot)	(P)
			P/O J H TIMMIS (Nav.)	(K)
			Sgt N F AXFORD (WOp/AG)	(K)
			Sgt J R ELLIOTT (AG)	(K)
27-Jul-42	AE267 PT-V	Hamburg	F/S A T JOHNSTONE (Pilot)	(K)
			W/O2 H N LAW (Navigator)	(K)
			P/O G E TILLING (WOp/AG)	(K)
			F/S J J PRICE (AG)	(K)
01-Aug-42	AE355 PT-A	Dusseldorf	W/O2 W J KAUFMAN (Pilot)	(K)
			W/O2 R R STEWART (Nav.)	(K)
			P/O W D FROST (WOp/AG)	(K)
			Sgt A J GREENAWAY (AG)	(K)

The signatures on the reverse of the Squadron Photograph (*see page 13*).

Several of the signatures may be matched to personnel mentioned in the text. F/Lt. S.J.Cybulski, DFC, RCAF (as he then was) died flying a Wellington of 156 Sqn to München on 21st December 1942; and F/O L.H.C.Gardiner, DFC, RCAF (as he then was) was killed navigating a 428 Sqn. Lancaster on a mission to Stettin on 30th August 1944. Both were from Ontario.

Sgt E.L. Trendell, DFM (*see page 43*) was later commissioned, reaching the rank of Flight-

49

Lieutenant on 5 April 1945. Two years later, the former Sgt. Frederick Arnold Melton also attained the rank of Flight-Lieutenant.

J.W.Bishop was also promoted and as a F/Lt. was awarded the DFC (*see page 41*). The absence of the names from casualty and PoW records suggests that he, along with F/Lts. Melton and Trendell, survived the war as free men.

It has not been possible to definitively locate Sgt.Endersby at 420 Squadron. It seems eminently possible, however, that the latter was Jack Stuart Endersby, who was promoted Sergeant in 1941, was later commissioned and, as Flight-Lieutenant J.S.Endersby, was killed navigating a Mosquito of 139 (Pathfinder) Squadron on 4th April 1945 (three weeks prior to the cessation of hostilities in Europe).

F/Lt. F.J.J.Champion, DFM (as he then was), later flew as a WOp/AG with 161 Squadron Hudsons out of Tempsford. On 27th November 1944, his aircraft was on an SOE mission (delivering or collecting agents over enemy territory) when it was shot down by a nightfighter. He, with the rest of the crew, is buried in Brussels Town Cemetery. His wife lived at Bracebridge Heath, Lincoln, near Waddington. He had won the DFM while serving with 420 Squadron (*see page 43*).

The Handley Page H.P. 52 HAMPDEN Mark 1

Specification

All-metal monoplane four-seater medium bomber; twin fins & rudders.

Two 1,000 h.p. Bristol Pegasus XVII 9-cylinder radial piston engines

Three-bladed de Havilland constant-speed airscrews

Max. Speed: 254 m.p.h at 13,800 feet.

Cruising Speed: 167 m.p.h. at 15,000 feet

Service Ceiling: 19,000 ft.

Range: 1,885 miles with 2,000 lb load

Weight (*empty*): 11,780 lb (*max. take-off*) 18,756 lb

Wingspan: 69ft. 2 in.

Length: 53ft. 7 in.

Height: 14ft.11in.

Wing Area: 668 sq.ft.

Fuel: Petrol, 654 gallons; oil, 36 gallons

The Handley Page HP53 **HEREFORD** was a variant of the Hampden, using 955-h.p. Napier Dagger XIII 24-cylinder H-type engines in place of the Pegasus. These proved unpopular: the engines were unreliable, seldom operating at normal temperature and consequently tending to self-destruct: they also produced an exhaust whine which was tiring as well as deafening. Only a few were used by operational squadrons: most went to OTUs, and some Herefords were converted "back" to Hampden specification.

44 Squadron Hampdens flying over Lincolnshire. The middle aircraft is AE202, KM-K

BIBLIOGRAPHY

The Good Die Never by Jean Barclay; published by Pamela Reid, 1993

Bomber Command Losses of the Second World War 1941 by W R Chorley; Midland Counties Publications, 1993: ISBN 0 904597 87 3

Bomber Command Losses of the Second World War 1942 by W R Chorley; Midland Counties Publications, 1994: ISBN 0 904597 89 X

The Hampden File by Harry Moyle; Air-Britain (Historians) Ltd, 1989: ISBN 0 85130 128 2

Hampden Special by Chaz Bowyer; Ian Allen Ltd, 1976: ISBN 0 7110 0683 0

The Handley Page Hampden by Philip J R Moyes; Profile Publications Ltd, 1965

Hampden Squadrons in Focus by Mark Postlethwaite; Red Kite, 2003: ISBN 0-9538061-6-2

Enemy Coast Ahead by Wing Cdr Guy Gibson VC; Michael Joseph Ltd, 1946

Handley-Page Hampden and Hereford Crash Log by Nicholas Roberts; Midland Counties Publications, 1980: ISBN 0-904597-34-2

The Bomber Command War Diaries by Martin Middlebrook and Chris Everett: first published by Viking Ltd, 1985: ISBN (Penguin paperback) 0-14-012936-7

The Hampden 1 Aeroplane Pilot's Notes published by the Air Council, 1939

The Crucible of War, 1939-1945 Vol 3 – The History of the Royal Canadian Air Force Squadrons by Brereton Greenhous, Stephen J Harris, William C Johnston and William GP Rawling; published by University of Toronto Press, 1994: ISBN 0-80-200574-8

The Thousand Plan *(The story of the first Thousand Bomber raid on Cologne)* by Ralph Barker, published by Chatto & Windus, 1965

The Founding of the Geology Department at Keele University: Memories of the first five intakes 1950-1958, ed. Thompson & Exley, published by the N. Staffs. Group of the Geologists Association of London, October, 2006

An Illustrated History of RAF Waddington 1916 - 1945 by Raymond Leach, Woodfield Publishing, 2003: ISBN 1-903953-44-8

Flight and the Aircraft Engineer magazine archive and the ***London Gazette*** archive.

Glossary

AC2	Aircraftman, Second Class
AG	Air Gunner
AOC	Air Officer Commanding
CO	Commanding Officer
DFC	Distinguished Flying Cross
DFM	Distinguished Flying Medal
DSO	Distinguished Service Order
F/Lt.	Flight-Lieutenant
F/O	Flying Officer
F/Sgt.	Flight-Sergeant
Flak	Anti-Aircraft fire *(abbreviation of German)*
Fw.	Feldwebel *(German:* = Sergeant)
Hptm.	Hauptman *(German:* = Captain (Flight Lieutenant))
Lt.	Leutnant *(German:* = 2nd Lieutenant (Pilot Officer))
Me.	Messerschmitt
Oblt.	Oberleutnant *(German:* = Lieutenant (Flying Officer))

Ofw.	Oberfeldwebel (*German*: = Warrant Officer)
OTU	Operational Training Unit
P/O	Pilot Officer
PoW	Prisoner of War
S/L	Squadron Leader
Sgt.	Sergeant
SOE	Special Operations Executive
Sqn	Squadron
Uffz.	Unteroffizer (*German*: = Corporal)
W/Cdr	Wing-Commander
W/O	Warrant Officer
W/Op	Wireless Operator
WOp/AG (W/AG)	Wireless Operator/Air Gunner

Compiled using Microsoft Word; set in Bookman Old Style typeface

www.ingramcontent.com/pod-product-compliance
Ingram Content Group UK Ltd.
Pitfield, Milton Keynes, MK11 3LW, UK
UKHW041433180426
11947UKWH00007B/425